A Simple Cup
Of
Coffee

A Simple Cup
Of
Coffee

Caroline Christian

authorHOUSE®

AuthorHouse™
1663 Liberty Drive
Bloomington, IN 47403
www.authorhouse.com
Phone: 1-800-839-8640

Published by AuthorHouse   11/16/2012

ISBN: 978-1-4772-9021-7 (sc)
ISBN: 978-1-4772-9020-0 (e)

Library of Congress Control Number: 2012921429

I dedicate this first book to my husband, Mike, who gave me faith and the opportunity to follow my dream. I couldn't ask for a better soulmate.

PROLOGUE

This story is not really about a cup of coffee. I mean, how boring would that be? It's really about a stupid cat. However, this stupid cat caused a major problem all because I wanted a 'simple cup of coffee'. Hence the title.

So, lets begin!

CHAPTER 1

Like most families these days, both my husband and I work full time jobs to keep up with today's expenses. We live a very busy life style having five children, which is why we allow ourselves twenty minutes every morning to relax over coffee before heading off to our respectful busy work days. I wasn't even down the stairs when I heard my daughter's loud screeching voice.

"Mom! Tell Brian to hurry up! I'm going to leave without him!"

"Alex, you need to drive your brother to school." I turned and yelled up the stairs myself. "Brian! Get a move on! Alex has to be at school earlier this morning!"

Alex is two years older than her brother. The mornings are always like this. She likes to be on time, where Brian is very lackadaisical, especially when it comes to school. After a fight and a half, a little yelling at my end and more screaming from my daughter, the two kids finally made it out the door. Too much for me to handle before my morning coffee.

"Let's drink our coffee outside!" I'm usually not this excited, or alert for that matter, so early in the morning. During my first cup of coffee, my head is usually lying down on the table with eyes shut. I'm far from being awake yet. Sometimes I think I can hear myself snoring. Once the first cup of java gets into me, I can start my second cup and almost be awake.

This particular morning found me desperately wanting to be outside. It was a beautiful spring morning. My husband and I did lots of work on the yard this weekend and I wanted to bask in the glow of our handy work. But when Mike doesn't want to do something, he comes up with excuses to try to justify his reasoning. "We can't have coffee outside, we have to go to work".

"Hon, what's the big deal? Either way, we have to go to work . . . drinking our coffee inside at the kitchen table or outside on the patio."

"So, what *is* the big deal?" he asks. "Why can't we just drink it inside? We'll throw burgers on the grill tonight and check out our handy work then. Besides, we won't be rushed."

"Mike, we just cleaned up the backyard, planted gorgeous flowers, mulched. Let's just relax outside with our coffee instead of inside. Please? I really want to see the results of all the hard work."

"Caroline, we're still in our pajamas. Actually, I'm in my underwear! We're not exactly dressed for the outdoors!"

Each morning before we come downstairs for our coffee, Mike has to throw on a pair of undies. He sleeps naked. Yep, no pajamas, not even underwear. He says he likes to 'breathe'. Another reason he sleeps 'sans clothing' is because he's hot all the time, so even with central air conditioning he sweats, even when he's just wearing shorts and a tee shirt.

Then there's me. A long sleeved thermal shirt and long 'comfy' pants, which this morning are my bright pink ones consisting of a ton of penny sized white polka dots. On top of that, I like to make sure my body is thoroughly covered and wrapped up with a sheet and a comforter. Then for good measure, I cuddle up with my 'blanky' that I crocheted myself about eight years ago. It's the warmest friggin blanket I own. Now mind you, I'm like this all year round. In the winter because it's clearly cold. But in the summer, as hot as it is, I freeze because we have central air in the house.

Every night, after bundling myself up like a cocoon, I roll over and snuggle up with Mike. The poor thing. He's sweating to begin with yet here I am wrapping myself all over him. He's so warm and comfy. Mike lets me fall asleep like this. Once asleep, which doesn't take long, he peels me off of him, blankets and all, then rolls to his side of the bed where he can then cool off and fall asleep himself.

I sleep straight through the night. A herd of elephants couldn't wake me up even if they stomped on top of me. Mike, on the other hand, could hear a toothpick roll off the kitchen table. That leaves him to be in charge of the alarm clock. He'll set it for 6:30. When it goes off at set time, he'll shut it off before the clock even thinks to make a second sound. Then he'll get up at seven on his own. I never hear a thing. Not that he gives me much time to hear the buzzing going off. If I was the one in charge of the alarm clock, it would ring for ten minutes before I would even know it existed. I'm so not a morning person.

Okay, where was I? Oh yeah. Mike doesn't want to go outside because according to his next excuse, someone will see him in his underwear. But I don't let that one fly past me. With my hands on my hips, my voice goes up an octave and I say to him, "Michael! The backyard is friggin fenced in! A six foot fence! Trust me! No one's looking!"

My husband finally gives in to me.

While Mike is pouring both our coffees, I'm picking up the pole that's jammed between the sliding door and the wall. I'm aware as most people are, that anyone can break into a house via sliding door. The locks on the sliders are never the best. Most people who have sliding doors drop a pole of some sort on the door's track, long enough to fit in tightly between the door and the wall so anyone trying to break in won't be able to move the door because of the pole itself.

I stand the pole up on the track against the wall and head outside. The patio table is inviting now that the debris and pollen had been cleaned off during yesterday's yard work. It's a glass coffee table, rectangular shape. There is no umbrella. We have two benches with backs, each with matching cushions. To finish the set are two chairs with the same matching cushions.

I fluff up the cushions on the chairs. Mike sits next to me and hands me my coffee. He knows exactly how I like it. First of all it needs to be strong coffee. French Roast is best. I like my coffee poured only three quarters or less in the cup. This helps the coffee cool down quicker so I can drink it fast. After all, I need to quickly get to that second cup of coffee. I like a hint of hazelnut coffee creamer and a touch of sweet-n-low. Thats how I like my coffee. Can you say "High Maintenance"? Mike drinks his coffee with lots of cream and one equal. Coffee filled to the top. He has one cup, and that gets him through the day. He's easy.

A hint of a smile crosses over my husband's face as he glances around the yard. He worked hard yesterday, and his face is now showing pride.

I couldn't believe I was able to get him out here this morning. Yesterday he could've cared less to look at his handy work. In fact, after yesterday, he didn't want to step foot outside again!

CHAPTER 2

Ten yards of cedar mulch were delivered on Saturday; dropped on our driveway. Yesterday, we lifted wheel barrel after wheel barrel of mulch out to the backyard. Because Mike was the one who did the majority of the mulch work, you can see the blisters on his palms and fingers. He's not fond of doing yard work. Mike would rather hire someone. He's a business man who works so hard during the week that he feels time with the family is worth more than the price you would pay to have someone mow your lawn. It's not like he never does yard work. During the spring and summer, he mows the lawn on occasion and once in a while he'll call in the pros. In the fall, he'll rake the leaves, and he'll shovel the snow in the winter. He's far from lazy. He just believes some things are better done by the professionals.

Together, we share the house work. Yes, it falls mostly on me, but he'll do the dishes after supper. He'll empty the dishwasher. When it's holiday time or I'm planning a party of some sort, Mike will hire someone to come and clean the house for me. This way I can concentrate on my party rather than worrying about the house. So grabbing a little professional help at times works for both of us.

However, we didn't want to hire anyone for this project. This was the yearly spring time "set up your backyard for the summer" make over. So we agreed that the two of us together could make a good day out of cleaning up the yard. But it was far from a 'good day' of yard work. The poor sole sweats when he sits in an air conditioned house, let alone outside on a hot, humid day. Not to mention that the pollen sends him into a new dimension. Needless to say, my husband complained left and right.

"We've been at it for hours! I've made about eighty trips back and forth with this mulch. I'm sweating!"

"Then why don't you take a break if you need one." I say this and mean it, knowing that the heat and pollen are getting to him.

"No! I just want to get this done and over with! This sucks!" And he says this quietly. Even when Mike yells, it's soft and calm, if that can even be possible.

All-righty then.

The distance from the driveway where the mulch was dumped to the fenced in backyard is about twenty feet. Once in the backyard, we have an area of about four hundred square feet. Though our backyard is bigger than that, there is an extension of the house that divides the backyard into two sections. Only one of these sections is fenced in. The mulch is being contained to this area, coming out as far as three feet from the fence. The area where the extension divides the backyard is where I wanted to plant some random flowers clustered within a generous amount of mulch.

He enters through the gate with another wheel barrel full of mulch. "Where else do you want it? This 'Fn' mulch is heavy!" (he used the actual four letter 'F' word, but my fingers weren't brave enough to type the real word into this story). He was now raising his voice at this point which he never does. We've both been at it for three hours.

Before lugging the mulch into the backyard, we had to move all the patio furniture to one side out of the way to make our work more efficient. Then we had to dig up the old mulch plus do lots of weeding. The weeding was a killer. Our patio is old. It is made up of large cement blocks of different shapes and sizes. The space in between each block was about an eighth of an inch thick give or take, allowing a lot of weeds to come through. A large gorgeous tree that was perched in the center of the patio has gigantic roots that are helping the cement blocks lift up off the ground's surface, enabling even more weeds to sneak through the cracks.

"Honey, why don't you put some more of the mulch over against the side of the house where I'm going to put the bird feeder. It will look nice." I was planting the flowers that we had picked up at Home Depot. My job was clearly a lot easier than his job. But he insisted on being the one to carry the mulch back and forth. He didn't want me to hurt myself.

"You already have some over there. It will be too much." (Remember what I told you about his excuses?)

"Hon, I'm going to put lots of plants in that area with the bird bath and bird feeder. I need more there."

Sweat's pouring down his face. "Well, I guess you don't want to mulch the front yard because you want more over there! We are going to run out of mulch without even touching the front yard!" He's gritting his teeth. And at this point, I'm biting my tongue. Why in God's name ask me where to put the mulch if you already know that you're not going to put it there?

I'm tired too. But we have a long way to go before finishing. "If you think it should go in the front yard, then by all means, put it in the front yard."

Apparently he didn't like that answer as he mumbles, "I need a break! I'm going to get some water!"

Sooooo, it wasn't quite the right time three minutes ago when I suggested a break. But now is a perfect time. Yep. Silly me.

Since the two of us have been working hard, we both took a break. We went into the cool, air conditioned house and sat at the table drinking ice cold bottled water. I must admit, it was refreshing. I definitely needed the break. I just didn't know it. He got up and splashed water on his face. He was working hard and sweating profusely. It's hard for me to truly understand his discomfort when I never get hot to begin with. When we're outside, I don't feel the heat like he does, so it's easy for me to keep going. In the meantime *his* body is shutting down.

After fifteen minutes of decompressing I glanced over at him and smiled, "Take your time babe. Just let me know when you're ready. I'm going to go out and continue to plant the flowers."

Without hesitation, and absolutely no grumpiness, Mike followed me outside. That little break did him wonders.

After adding a little more mulch to the area that I earlier had asked of him, he disappeared into the front yard to lay the rest of the mulch. Two hours later, we were finished.

And in the end, he worked hard and it payed off. Until the next morning.

CHAPTER 3

"Now isn't this beautiful babe?", I ask him, while we're sipping coffee, glancing around at the newly planted flowers. Apple Blossoms are off to the right, aligning with the side of the house. There are also some behind us, the stem buried under the freshly laid mulch. Azaleas are starting to peek through to our left. They were already in the ground from when we bought the house a year ago. Begonias are set off to the right of us in a gorgeous cluster that I knew would bring vibrant color to the yard.

Behind us to the left are Bluebells and Lilies, which were already coming up thanks to the previous owners. They also planted Impatiens around the tree, which stands proudly behind us with it's large green leaves. Many tulips, which I planted myself, are scattered randomly around the yard, mostly up against the fence. All in a palette of assorted colors to add an energetic feel to the yard.

"Nice underwear," I smile at him as he sits next to me. He puts his bare feet up on the table. All of his 'glory' is hanging out of his underwear. He doesn't seem to care. Goes to show you that the 'everybody will see me in my underwear' remark that he made back in Chapter 1 was just an empty excuse.

I slurp my coffee loudly. "Oh my God this coffee is soooo good. You made it perfect today!"

"You say that every morning. Your coffee could taste like mulch and you'd still tell me how good it tastes." He says that to me as he's staring at the cedar mulch that he worked so hard on yesterday.

I look up at him and smile. He's right about the coffee. Sort of. I know a bad cup of coffee when I taste it, but he truly makes a perfect cup. "You know, a little mulch in the coffee wouldn't be so bad if it was *me* who made it. It would probably improve the taste."

He laughs. All our family members joke at how badly I make coffee. I'm a *huge* coffee drinker, and I like it strong. So when I make coffee, I always add an extra scoop or two, or three just to be sure it's strong enough. And per usual, it tastes horrible. Almost on the muddy side. Mike makes it perfect all the time. Every time the family is over to visit, I'll ask them if they want me to make a pot of coffee. They say 'Sure, but only if Mike makes it.'

We both glance around the yard. "It does look nice," Mike says. "You were right about that area of plants. It looks great. Sorry about being a pain in the ass yesterday." And he means it when he says it.

We continue commenting on the great job we did. As we are talking we notice Mittens, our seven month old kitten playing with something near the sliding door. I'm giggling while watching her. She's so damn cute. Mittens is really my daughter's cat.

Alexandra is the oldest of our five children. I have two children through my first marriage. Alex is eighteen. Blonde hair, blue eyes, she stands about my height, five foot two inches. Struggled in school because it wasn't cool to be smart. She gave me a hard time from age twelve until about seventeen. Typical teenager. But now she got her act together. She's determined to go to college. She's a good kid.

Brian is sixteen. Never gave me a hard time like my daughter did, until recently. I think he's hitting the 'teenage years' a little later than most. He's very tall, standing about six feet. Dark brown hair with blue eyes. He too, is a good kid. But aren't they all.

Mike has three kids from his first marriage. Aaron is the oldest at age eight. Blonde hair, blue eyes and a little small for his age. Emily and Sara are six year old fraternal twins. With gorgeous red hair, Emily is a spitting image of her father. She's tall for her age with blue eyes like her brother. Sara has blonde hair and is the smallest of the three. She too has blue eyes. All three kids are very well behaved.

Back in November Alex was begging me for a kitten. I told her 'no' that we already had a cat and a dog. "Please mommy?" Calling me 'mommy' was her way of being 'cutesy' and knowing she would make me melt. It was 'Mom' on an everyday basis; 'Mum!' when she was angry. So now, Alex got 'mommy's' attention.

"Kittens grow up to be cats, Alex. It's a lot to take care of a pet. They are cute when they're little, but there is a lot of responsibility. If I allow you to have this kitten, it will be up to you to feed it, clean up after it, and even pay for the vet visits." I've softened enough to the point where she knew she won me over. I guess part of me wanted a kitten as well. Mike, on the other hand, did not. He was away on business. I called and asked him if Alex could get the kitten and he immediately said 'no'. We already had one cat and a dog. We didn't need anymore animals. When he came home from his trip, there was a new member of the family. Her name was Mittens.

I know, I know. Total disrespect on my part. It was something I should have talked to my husband about first. Obviously Mike wasn't happy. He just told me that the kitten would now be mine to take care of, not his. Because God knows that Alex, a teenager, would not take the full responsibility that she should for *her* cat. Of course, once again, my husband was right.

Mittens is a female calico cat (kitten). The temperament of this breed of cat is standoffish and snobbery. I was disappointed when Alex brought her home. A) because she lied to me. The kitten she was getting was *supposedly* a black rescue kitty that they were going to put down, and B) I despise calicos because of their behavior. Nonetheless, Mittens is here and here she stays.

So, here we are, my husband and I, chatting about our day to come, what's for dinner, what's up for the week, do we have upcoming plans for the weekend, etc.

"Do you think your day will be busy?", he asks. It's the usual first words he says to start our morning conversation. I'm far from a morning person, so conversation is not my highlight until I'm on my second cup of coffee. So he begins our day with simple questions. Questions he knows

I'll be able to answer and aren't really that important. He's wide awake, alert and attentive twenty-four-seven.

"I'm going to be wicked busy today but that makes the day fly, so that's a good thing." I'm a Graphic Designer. It's a fun job, but everything is deadline sensitive. So working long days to get material out to the printer is never unheard of. At the end of the day, Mike and I are usually home about the same time.

As we sip our coffee and discuss our upcoming day we notice Mittens at the door. She's adorable, playing around with the pole that I leaned up against the door frame earlier. Being a kitten, she's curious about everything and feels it's important to play with anything and everything that comes into view at any moment. Mike and I smile at her cuteness.

"I'm planning to make chicken for dinner tonight. Sound okay to you?"

He looks at me and smiles. "Anything you're in the mood to cook is fine with me."

Mike will try anything I put in front of him. He'll be honest and let me know if it's a favorite or if he wasn't thrilled with it. He'd be happy to eat macaroni and cheese every night. But I like to have something different. Not only do I enjoy cooking, but I love to eat and experience different foods in all different ways. It's no wonder I'm not six hundred pounds!

As if we were reading each others mind, we both look over at the sliding door where Mittens continues to play with the pole. Suddenly the pole drops. In the track. I think.

Mike's not thinking happy thoughts as he's putting together what just happened. "So are you thinking what I'm thinking? Is it possible that the pole is actually in the track?"

I'll admit to you that I was a tad worried but I sure as hell didn't admit that to him.

I was lucky enough to get his ass out here this morning. We were relaxed, it was a gorgeous morning, and I didn't want to turn it into a disaster. Which became just that. A disaster.

CHAPTER 4

Okay. So we are sitting outside on our patio enjoying our newly landscaped backyard, sipping our morning coffee before heading off to our busy work days. Sound good? Of course it does. It truly was how it started out. A quick twenty minutes outside on our patio before work drinking coffee. But then came Mittens. The new cat that Mike didn't want.

I'm sure he heard the worrisome in my voice. "Let's just finish our coffee and then I'll go check the door. I'm sure the cat didn't knock the pole directly in the track. I mean, what are the chances of that?"

Shit! I could tell I didn't sound convincing.

"Yeah, probably not," he says. Mike truly sounded convinced! I mean, what *were* the chances?

"Do you have any meetings today?"

He shrugs his shoulders. "Yep. I've got a meeting at nine, which is just with my group, then another at eleven. That one's probably going to last an hour. It's with all upper management. I have one at two-thirty then my last meeting is at three." He say's this like it's an easy day because there are only four meetings.

Mike is a Managing Director at an insurance company. He oversees four separate teams. One of those teams is in Canada. A total of sixty-two people report to him. It's a stressful job, but he worked hard to get where he is.

"Well, that's not bad." My response is not genuine because I'm still worried about the door. You see, if that pole fell directly in the track, we will be locked out of the house. That wouldn't be pretty.

He looks at me and asks while handing me his cup, "Do you mind getting us a second cup of coffee? You were right. It's relaxing out here and I am quite impressed that we pulled this off like we did. The yard looks beautiful!"

"Sure! No problem!" His happy tone has now convinced me that all is good. I'm just going to go right on in the house. That sliding door is going to open up no problem. And I'm going to come back out with two more delicious cups of coffee. And we will enjoy our handy work for another five minutes, because that's about all the time we have left. Then we have to get our butts in fifth gear so we can make it to work on time. No worries.

I take his coffee cup and walk over (for some reason, very slowly) to the sliding glass door. Without looking down at the track through the door, (I don't seem to want to do that for fear of what I'll see) I just pull at the door handle. And it doesn't seem to budge. *Shit!* Now I glance down at the track. *Shit!* The pole is actually fully in the track! *Shit! Shit! Shit!*

I take a breath, turn around and head back to Mike. "I'm just going to put these cups on the table. I can't seem to open the door with my hands full."

What an idiotic, asinine, totally unconvincing, worse excuse EVER that anyone in the world (even Mike), can EVER make. Even the excuses that kids make for not doing homework, married couples for committing adultery, drunk drivers speaking to a cop, (you get the picture). *Shit!* The door won't open. Period. End of story. Coffee cups being in or out of my hand, the door is NOT going to open. *Shit!*

My husband eyes me. "The pole is in the track, isn't it." This does not come out of his mouth as a question. It's a statement.

I put on a seriously fake smile. "Yeah, but I'm sure it's not stuck."

I go back to the door and pull at the handle again. Nothing. Now I try pulling it hard. Nothing. I try a different approach. Gently, very gently. Nothing. Now I'm pulling, twisting, banging, all at the same time. Nothing.

And through all of this, that stupid cat is sitting on the other side of the door looking at me. Staring. As if to say, "Are you coming in or not?" *Shit!*

CHAPTER 5

"You gotta be kidding me." Mike is now standing next to me looking down at the pole that has momentarily locked us out of our house. "Let me try."

Now if at any other time Mike would've say something like that, I would have been like, 'yeah, if YOU pull the handle it will open because YOU pull handles better than I do.' But at this point, I'm desperate for anything! If I found a squirrel right now scurrying up the tree I'd ask *him* to give it a whirl!

My husband's not happy. Seriously for good reason. "Look at the stupid cat! She's staring at us like we are a couple of idiots!" He gives the door handle one last yank. To no surprise it doesn't budge. (I swear that Mittens just laughed at him). Mike goes back and sits down on the chair.

I calm myself down and decide it's time to try a different approach. I bend down and look at Mittens, who has decided to make full eye contact with me. She's seriously wondering what our problem is. I hate her.

"Now Mittens. Listen to Mama. Play with the pole again." I say this while tapping at the bottom of the door where the pole sits. Stuck. Tightly. *Shit*! "Come on kitty. Pull at the pole. You can get it." Again, Mittens is just staring at me with those big green eyes. She is soooo not cute right now.

Alex would always say, "Isn't Mittens cute? Look at her?" And Mike has this on going joke where his reply is always, "Alex, she is not cute. She's ugly." Well, right now, Mittens is far from cute, let me tell you.

I'm still trying to teach Mittens how to pick up the pole when Mike says, "Seriously Caroline? You think that's going to work? While you're at it, ask her if she'll pour us a second cup of coffee! Make sure she puts extra cream in mine! Will you tell her that?" Mike is saying this sans smile. Nil. None. Definitely a face that's not happy. And he's right. 'Cuz there's Mitt, staring at me saying "Dumb Ass".

I deserve it.

I go back and sit with Mike. "Oh my God, hon. What are we going to do? We are legit, locked out of the house!"

He looks a little calmer. "While you were playing '*how to train your kitty to lift a three foot pole over her head*', I came up with an easy answer to all of this. Your kids always leave the front door unlocked. We panicked for nothing."

Oh my God, he was right. Every morning my kids are fighting with each other on their way out of the house to go to school. As much as I remind them to lock the door, they never do because of all the drama! I gave Mike a hug and smiled.

Mike is a very calm guy. I have never seen him panic and he never gets angry. If he's upset about something he talks about it. He's the type that thinks things through. He always comes up with a solution before he has time to stress out. He's the only one in his family without high blood pressure.

I look into his beautiful blue eyes. "I'll run out front and let us in!"

Oh, thank God! I was so panicked that it didn't even cross my mind at first. Leave it to Mike to come up with the answer. He was so right. My kids never lock the doors. Whether we are home or not, whether they are fighting or not, they leave the doors unlocked all the time. Ahhhh, so easy. I stressed for nothing.

Mike gets up and stands by the slider to wait for me while I go open the front door. I run through the gate, close it tightly and get to the front steps. I swing open the stormer then I turn the door knob. *Shit!* I try the knob again. *Shit!*

My husband sees me through the back door shrugging his shoulders like 'what's the problem?' type of shrug. He motions me to try again, making a half fist and turning his hand as if he's holding a door knob. Because let's make it very clear. You see, my husband KNOWS how to open a door and I DON'T! So maybe I'll just buy that book called 'OPENING DOORS FOR DUMMIES'! *Shit!*

I'm staring at his hand motions. Yeah, I'll jiggle it to the right side three times, then jiggle it to the left side twice, then three more jiggles to the right, and that should open the door! IT'S NOT OPENING! IT'S LOCKED!

I'm yelling this at him through the glass of my door and his door. Problem is, I'm really yelling it, not mouthing it. I probably woke up the neighbors. *Shit!*

After all my yelling, I still give the door knob one last try for good measure. Obviously nothing happens. The door is clearly locked. On the bright side, I just saved myself fifteen bucks. I no longer need a book that teaches me how to open doors.

I can see Mike going back to sit down. As I'm looking through the glass, a movement to my right makes me jump back. It's Mittens. She must have heard me at the door. She's sitting up on a table that we have next to the front door. The table is positioned under a window. She's staring at me with her eyes blinking as if to say, 'Why aren't you coming inside?'. And what do I do? I point to the door knob and motion with my hand to try to teach her how to open the door. God, I *am* a Dumb Ass!

I go back through the gate and sit with Mike. I'm staring at the two empty cups of coffee. "I could really use a second cup of coffee." He looks at me with his mouth gaped open and right there and then I know to zip it. It was my dumb idea to come out here in the first place. What was I thinking? I mean if I just listened to him earlier. He said we could have a barbecue tonight and eat outside. But no. I need to have COFFEE outside. Dumb Ass.

"You know," he says. "Brian always unlocks the bathroom window. Why don't we go see if that's open. Just a thought."

He's right! My son has gone through like five keys since we've lived here. He loses them all the time. We've only been here a little over a year and I can't tell you how many keys we've given that kid. So we got to the point where we stopped making keys for him. What Brian does, is he leaves windows unlocked so he can climb through when he gets home from school. Now, I know what you're thinking. Why not have a hidden key outside somewhere for the family in case of emergencies (like the mess we're in right now)? We did have keys hidden in plants, under rocks, above the doors, etc. But my son would always take those keys and lose them as well. Hence the open windows.

So I run around the beautifully mulched, copious display of flowers and through the tiny gate that will lead me to the other half of the backyard where the downstairs bathroom window is located. Sure enough, there is a chair perched under the window, as if my son had planned on climbing through the window after school today! Alleluia!

"Mike, you're right! I think it's unlocked! Oh! Thank God!" I'm screaming, I'm so excited. It's after eight o'clock and we are both going to be late for work as is, never mind the fact that we still haven't showered yet.

I climb onto the chair and put my palms against the window. I press against the glass of the window. I'm trying to slide it upward while I push, but nothing seems to be happening. Hmm. Well, maybe my hands are too sweaty. I wipe my hands on my polka dotted bottoms and try again. Hmm. Maybe I shouldn't push so hard. I'll just try to slide the window up without pushing. Yeah. That will work.

I hear Mike from across the way. We can't see each other because the kitchen's extension is dividing us. He's on the fenced in side that we 'landscaped' yesterday, and where the sliding door to the kitchen is located. "Everything okay? Did you get it open yet?"

"Give me a second, babe." I do believe those words were said through gritted teeth. I'm trying not to yell. It's my fault that we're locked out of the house to begin with, so Mike doesn't deserve my anger.

I try to open the window again, but nothing budges so much as a hair. *Shit!* It's got to be unlocked! *Shit!*

"Caroline, are you there? I didn't hear you. Did you get it open?"

What the 'Fu—'!! Really? I'm starting to lose it. I'm no longer in 'nice' mode.

"No babe. I didn't get it open. I could use your help." I said this nicely, but with a raised voice.

My God, I'm taking it out on him. But it's me who wants to start our day with a simple cup of coffee; it's me who wanted to start this morning's coffee outside; and it's me who allowed my daughter to bring that stupid cat home.

My hands are now by my side and it's my head that's banging against the window ever so gently. *Thwap, Thwap, Thwap.* I've given up.

CHAPTER 6

During this entire fiasco my favorite word became 'Shit'. I'm usually not like that, but this was just getting too much. My husband was calmer than I was. I felt bad that I yelled at him when in fact, this whole incident is *my* fault because I just had to have my coffee outside! God, I suck!

Mike comes over to the side of the house where he finds me standing up on the chair. He sees me banging my head against the window. "The window is locked." He asks this but not with a question. It's more a statement. When he said it, I could hear a hint of hope in his voice. That maybe I just couldn't open it. That all he will have to do is have a bit of a stronger grip and slide that bad boy up. That the window was indeed unlocked. That once opened I'll be able to climb through the window, fall directly into the porcelain tub, ending up with a big egg on my head along with a bruised knee cap because it's a long drop. I'll painfully climb over the tub, out the bathroom door, into the kitchen, remove the 'Fu—' pole and save the day.

Can you say *Fantasy Land*? Cuz that's the world I'm living in right now. It's not happening. The window is locked and I have to blame someone so I blame my kids. After all, they always leave the front door unlocked. The downstairs bathroom window is always unlocked. But 'NO'! Not today! For some Godly reason my kids chose to listen to their mother and lock the doors, and not climb through the windows. Today. TODAY! I mean, WHAT WERE THEY THINKING?! Damn kids.

Mike and I walk back to our seats to allow a minute of moping. One needs to go through 'mopeville land' to get it off their chest before moving on. So that's what we did. "You didn't have to get mad at me, you know. I just asked you a question." He was talking about when I told him I could use his help trying to open the window.

"Honey, you asked me like three times if I got the window open. Don't you think that if I managed to open it you would be the first to know? Don't you think I would have come to the sliding door to let you in? Or do you think I would have just disappeared upstairs and taken my shower first, *before* letting you in? Seriously."

"I only asked you twice." A couple of minutes later, he lifts his head and says, "What about Chickie?"

Oh my God! I can't believe it. Chickie has a key! Why didn't we think of that before? Well, actually, let me explain ourselves before you think of us as complete idiots. (Okay, it's a little late for that . . .) It's not that we didn't think about it. It's just that it wasn't necessary to come up with that idea just yet. Technically, we've only been locked outside for like fifteen minutes. Our first thought was the front door. We truly thought the door would be unlocked. When that didn't work, we tried the window. In our minds, those were the easiest solutions. So even though it took a full chapter to take you through those events, calling Chickie is literally only our third attempt (with the exception of teaching Mittens how to lift three foot poles over her head).

Chickie is a friend of ours that lives in our neighborhood; about two thirds of a mile down the street. We know her from our bowling league. She found out we lived in Canton and told us she had just bought a house here. Sure enough, it happened to be right around the corner. Chickie loves animals. She takes care of our pets when we are on vacation. We gave her a permanent key because on random occasions, she'll want to walk the dog and we are usually at work. She's in her early sixties and retired. It works for all of us because A) It makes Chickie happy to see the little critters, B) the animals are happy to see Chickie, and C) Mike and I are happy because we know we don't have to rush home for fear that the dog may leave some of his 'business' in piles on the kitchen floor, or that he'll go number 'onezees' leaving it seeping into the carpets. Yeah, I'd say it's a win-win giving Chickie a key to the house.

Anyway, back to making that phone call. I happened to have my cell phone with me. I was taking pictures of the patio's gorgeous surroundings when we first stepped outside this morning. (God, that seems like hours ago.) So as luck would have it, the phone was sitting on the patio table. Hey, maybe this means our luck is going to change! Wouldn't that be great?!

I dialed Chickie's number letting it ring only once. Hmm. No answer. "You barely let it ring!", says Mike, surprised at how quickly I hung up the phone.

"I know, but what if she's still sleeping?" I hate waking people up too early in the morning. I, myself, am not a morning person.

For the second time this morning my husband's mouth drops open. "Hello! Who cares? Look at us! We need to be rescued! Besides, she's a morning person. She's probably awake. Try letting it ring more than once and maybe, just maybe, she'll have time to answer the phone!".

He's right. Though needing to be 'rescued' is a little harsh. I would just say we need a little assistance.

I dial her number again. This time I let it ring ten times. I actually counted. But still, no answer. "Maybe I dialed the wrong number. I could have dialed her cell phone number and she never answers that. She uses that for emergencies only. Let me just try again."

Once again, I'm pushing for some luck. I'm grasping at hope. I look through my phone's address book and double check her number and I positively ID the correct digits for her house number before pressing the call button. In the meantime Mike has now gotten up and he is pacing. He is no longer hoping. The only thing he's grasping at are what's hanging out of his underwear. And he doesn't care who sees. Take that fence down! Who cares!

Mike knows that Chickie is not going to answer. My husband is tired of waiting. He still needs to shower, get dressed and go to work. He's starting to work up a sweat. He's running out of time. Because after all, Caroline wanted to have one 'simple cup of coffee' OUTSIDE. (I know this is what he's thinking.) ARE YOU LOVING THE OUTDOORS NOW, CAROLINE?! GORGEOUS, ISN'T IT?! I swear to God I can hear him thinking it. If I were him I'd be saying it out loud, right at me. But he never yells at me though, God bless him.

I let the phone ring until it went to voice mail. I left a brief message letting her know that her services are needed ASAP, to call us when she has the chance. Then I plop my ass down on the seat cushion and glance over at the sliding glass door. My God. It's Mittens staring at us. *Bitch!*

I jump out of the seat and run over to the door. "Come on you stupid cat! Pick up the damn pole! Just take it out of the track! How difficult can it possibly be? It's just a pole, for the love of God!"

I sound ridiculous even to myself. I can hear my senseless words coming out of my crackpot of a head before they even reach my lips. To top it off, Mitt is just sitting there. She hasn't even moved during my tantrum. She's sitting up tall with her head held high like she's proud. *Proud!* She's even blinking her eyes as if to say, 'I just can't be bothered with such foolishness'. What a *bitch!*

I go back to sit next to Mike. He totally moved to the other side of the table. Apparently he thinks I'm a wack job too. I don't blame him. Once again, for the third, fourth, maybe even fifth time this morning, his mouth is dropped open in disbelief. Now I know why he's taking all this better than me. I've lost control. He's never seen me like this and he knows that someone should be calm. He opted for himself, seeing that I'm coming close to wearing a straight jacket. Okay then. I'll take a deep breath and just think.

"Sorry about that babe. While I was having my nervous break down, did you come up with any other solutions?"

"Are you sure no one in your family has a key?" Now I can hear the disquieting in his voice. He's not really calm. He's troubled. He's not the type to give up, but that's how it's coming out of his voice. I'm feeling bad.

"I've never given my family a key. They're hardly ever over. I never thought for once to give them a key. I'm sorry."

"But honey, your family lives ten houses down the street. Why wouldn't you just give them a key for emergency situations, say, like this one?" Mike says it so placidly. It makes me feel that much more guilty.

"Do you need to call work? Use my phone and let them know you're going to be late. Cuz even if Chickie calls us back, there's no way you'll get to work on time for the first meeting." I hand him my cell phone. He makes the call to work explaining that he's running late. He canceled the meeting with his group, but said nothing more. Just that he'll be in as soon as he can.

I suppose I should call work too. Instead I wait, because I just work down the street. You never know; maybe

Chickie will get back to us soon. I glance around the yard. Man am I bummed. I mean, putting a key under the rock seemed like the only thing we had to do when we first moved in. If at anytime we needed someone to go into our house while we weren't home, we would just let them know where that key was located. Of course after like *ten* keys disappeared (thank you Brian), we decided not to put one outside anymore.

Mike's parents have a key to our house. But they live an hour away. A lot of good that would do. Now you're thinking why on earth would we give them a key and not my family. Especially since they live so far away. Well, it was nothing personal. First of all, his parents flat out asked us for a key. No problem. We gave them one. Second of all, Mike and I would come home from work and find surprises from his parents. Like, the bathroom painted, the kids' rooms redecorated, the lawn mowed, etc. They were retired and thought they would do what they could to help us out, especially when we first moved in and we didn't have time to finish up the redecorating of the house. But calling them for help at this time in the morning, while they live an hour away, just wouldn't help our situation. *Shit!*

Okay, so time for plan C. Or is it D? E? F? God, I can't even count anymore.

"I know she's in school, but I'm going to call Alex." I say this with uncertainty. I sure as hell don't know what I'm going to ask her, or what my plan is, but she's got a key. That's all I know at this point.

Mike is thinking the same thing. "And what exactly are you going to ask her to do? She's in school!".

"Do you have any other thoughts? You're the one who came up with all the ideas so far. And all of them were the perfect answer. They made so much common sense that I would have bet my life on each and every one of them, that they would, indeed, get us back into the house. But here we are. Still in our morning getups, trying to get back into our own home. So, I ask you again. Do you have any better ideas?"

"Call Alex."

CHAPTER 7

So, that was that. I picked up my phone and dialed my daughters cell phone number. I knew that kids weren't supposed to have their cell phones on, or with them for that matter, during school hours. But what the heck. What teenager ever listens to the rules. (Oh wait! Mine do. *Today! Today* they locked all the doors and windows like I asked them to! Thanks guys! Love yas!) It rang about ten times before going to voice mail. I didn't leave a message. I looked through my phone's address book and found the school's number. I dialed that. The secretary picked up on the third ring. "Good morning. May I help you?"

Oh boy. I mean, sure, this is great. I have someone on the phone. But as mentioned earlier, I had no plan. So what do I say? *Shit!*

I decided to start with the truth. I've always told my kids that when in doubt, just tell the truth. Otherwise things just escalate and get worse. Well, the truth I'm about to reveal is pretty embarrassing. But do I have a choice? I'll keep it simple. Maybe I won't have to get into details.

"Ahem. My name is Caroline. I'm looking for my daughter, Alexandra. I'm not sure what room she's in at this time. It's important that I speak with her."

"Sure, no problem. May I put you on hold for just a second please?" She sounded pleasant.

"Sure." Well, that wasn't too bad. I didn't have to get personal. I would have sounded like such a moron! Can you imagine?

"Hello. This is Jean Welch. I'm sorry to have made you wait. With whom am I speaking with again?"

Oh boy. I give her our full names and repeat what I had told her earlier. "Yes, it's rather important that I speak with her."

Okay. Again, not so bad.

"Mrs. Benson, what grade is your daughter in?"

"Oh, yes, I'm sorry. She's a senior." I'm failing to give Ms. Welch any and all the information she actually needs because I'm so nervous that I'll give away my disconcerting situation. The poor woman has to pull teeth to practically get me to speak.

"All the seniors are outside filing into the buses. Today is their final field trip before school ends. I'm not sure I'll be able to catch her in time, Mrs. Benson."

Shit! Time for the humiliation. I was hoping it didn't have to come to this.

"Ms. Welch, I really need my daughter's help at this point. My husband and I are locked out of our house and she's got the only key. Is there any chance at all that you can reach her before the buses leave the parking lot?" Phew! No need for full explanation. We're simply locked out of the house. It happens to everyone. No big deal.

"Mrs. Benson, I can probably get to her before the buses leave but she won't be able to drive home to let you in the house and get back here in time to make the bus for her trip. If I can find which bus she's on and we're lucky enough that she has her keys with her and not in her locker, I'll be more than happy to drive them to your home. Will that work for you?"

Good God! Is there really someone that nice that lives on this planet? You've got to be kidding me! We could be saved!

"Mrs. Benson? Are you there. We're running out of time."

"Yes! Yes! Oh, that would be great." I'm beside myself with merriment!

"Why don't you give me your number and I'll call you right back. Are you calling from your cell phone, or a neighbors house?"

"Umm, it's my cell phone." I give her my number and we hang up.

I turn to my husband. His eyes are full of questions that I have no problem filling in with answers. Before he even asks, I'm all over it.

"Oh my God! She's going to call me back. She's running outside to try to stop the buses to see if she can find Alex and hopefully she'll have her keys on her and then she'll drive them over to our house! Can you believe it? How thoughtful is that?"

For like the sixth time this morning (I'm all done counting anything at this point. It's pure guess work.), Mike's mouth is wide open with his chin practically touching his knees. "You need to slow down. Who's calling you back? Why is Alex on a bus somewhere? Who's keys? And who's coming over?"

Yeah. Everything I just said made no sense. I took a deep breath and spoke slowly and clearly. "Alex has her final senior field trip. We talked about it last night over dinner, remember? And that's why she was yelling at Brian to hurry up this morning. Okay, well she always yells at Brian in the morning. But anyway, with everything going on this morning, I completely forgot about it. Alex is on one of the three buses that are leaving for the trip. The buses are about to leave. Now, the secretary, her name is Jean Welch, is going to see if she can find which bus Alex is on. Alex will hopefully have her house key with her. If she does, she'll give it to Ms. Welch. Ms. Welch said she'll be glad to drive it over to us." Phew!

My husband nods his head with understanding. He looks to be a tad hopeful, but doesn't want to be too optimistic . . . just in case. "And if Alex *doesn't* have her keys with her? What if she left them in her locker?"

I put my phone back on the table. "Well, that's the thing. The buses are literally just about to leave. If Alex's keys are in her locker, I don't think she'll have time to get them to give to Ms. Welch. Either way Ms. Welch will call us back . . . Either with good news or bad news. But she'll call us back. Let's hope it's good news."

With this said, I stand up and walk back to the sliding door. Mittens is back. She's so proud of herself for what she's done. She's not sure what she did, but she knows it's all about her and that's what's important to this cat. My other cat, Seymore, could care less. He's an orange tiger cat and just goes with the flow. Gets along with everyone. He wouldn't dream of locking us out of the house!

God, listen to me! Okay, so Mittens probably didn't purposely do this either, but if you look at her, just look at how she's staring back at us, it's almost as if she did it for a laugh. I mean, she's *smiling*! I swear! This whole thing is funny to her!

WHY ISN'T MS. WELCH CALLING ME BACK!

I go back to the table and grab the phone to turn up the volume. As I do this, I notice that I missed a call! WHAT? Are you shit'n me? I look to see if there is a voice mail, and sure as shit there is one.

"Oh my God! Didn't you hear this ring, Mike?" I'm back to yelling at him, even though he's done absolutely nothing wrong. Turning my phone over, I notice the ringer is off. Oh, that's just *PISSA*! I always turn it off before I go to bed at night, and I hadn't turned it back on this morning. I usually don't need to. I switch it back on and I listen to the voice mail.

"Hello Mrs. Benson. This is Jean Welch. Hopefully I don't have the wrong number. I found your daughter and she gave me her house key. If you could call me back to let me know how to proceed that would be great. I believe you have the school's number."

God! How could I be so stupid! Who leaves the ringer off when they're expecting a call?

I SUCK! What was Mittens calling me earlier? Oh, yeah. *A Dumb Ass*!

(Now I think cats can speak. Can you say *Neurologist*?)

"God, Hon. What an empty-headed loser I am! I can't believe I missed her call!"

"Caroline, call her back. You need to calm down. She left a message, right? What did she say?"

Oh. Geez. "You're right. She said she got the key. She told me to call her. Sorry babe. I *do* need to calm down."

I dialed the school's number. "Good morning. May I help you?" It was Ms. Welch!

"Hi! It's Caroline Benson! I'm so sorry I missed your call. My ringer was off. Isn't that silly?" I sounded like a boob.

"It's okay. Alex gave me her house key. So all is good. Would you like me to drop it off to you?"

Sweet Jesus. I love her and I've never met her. "Are you sure you don't mind? I mean, can you do that? I don't want to put you out of your way."

Of all the stupid things to say. First off, of course I want her to go out of her way! I need the key! Second, the poor woman not only came up with the idea of dropping my daughter's key off to me, at my front door, but she's already gone out of her way searching for my daughter, in what was surely a top speed chase that I'm sure Ms. Welch did not have on her schedule for first thing this morning. (I hope she wore sneakers.)

And I choose now to ask her if she doesn't mind going out of her way? God, I suck!

"It's no problem. Where do you live? I'll come right now." She's so sympathetic. Imagine what she'd think if she knew how we got locked out of the house. I give her our address and thank her repeatedly.

"Phewwwww! Finally! As you put it, we're saved!" I plop down on the chair like I just ran three miles. "What a morning. I'm so sorry, babe."

"Don't apologize yet, sweetie. We're still sitting outside. Until I get my butt in that shower, I'm going to keep believing that we're stuck out here. I hate to be the pessimist, but let's face it . . . nothing has gone our way yet this morning. With the exception that you got to have a nice cup of coffee while admiring some stupid plants."

"All right, all right. All I wanted was a simple cup of coffee outside. Who'd have thunk it would have turned out like this? And what were the chances of Mittens dropping that pole in the track like that? You've got to admit, it's pretty funny, this whole thing."

"Do you really think, at this very moment, I'm finding anything funny? Ask me like five months from now and maybe, just maybe I can laugh about it. Again, we're still not inside the house yet."

He's right though. I can't even laugh right now. I'm still pissed at that cat. God, over the last forty-five minutes I have been angry with my son, my daughter, and even Mike. But most of all, I'm so infuriated with myself. I know it will turn out to be funny someday. Hopefully sooner than later.

He looked at me and gave me half a grin. "You and your damn coffee. Great idea, babe. Glad you thought of it. Let's do it again tomorrow."

It did sound like a good idea at first, but boy did that backfire. It's just that how can something so tranquil turn into the most tormenting morning ever? I wouldn't dare ask him to have coffee outside with me again. I'd be afraid of what would happen. I can't even imagine. Telling *this* story to anyone is embarrassing enough. Like who would believe it, anyway?

"Caroline, the high school's not that far away. She could be here any minute. I don't know about you, but I sure as hell don't want to miss her when she pulls in the driveway. That's all we need, is for her to turn around because we weren't out front to greet her."

"I'm with ya!" I jump up, grab my phone and give him a smile. "Are you sure you don't want to go out front and get the key from her? You look rather sexy in that underwear of yours."

"It's all yours, babe. I'll just sit here and wait for you to come through that sliding glass door." He says it pointing fiercely at the slider.

CHAPTER 8

I go out front to the driveway to wait for Jean Welch. I'm so relieved. I lean against my car twiddling my thumbs. While looking at my fingers I can't help but notice my bright pink pajama bottoms covered with hundreds of white polka dots. Could I look any more ridiculous? These bottoms are noticeable a mile away! She's going to think I'm some kind of bonehead. Not that she doesn't already.

Jean Welch pulls in the driveway. Thank God! I walk over to her car with my hands crossed over my tee shirt, secretly trying to cover my free swinging boobs with my arms (I'm not wearing a bra). At the same time I'm trying to figure out how I can cover my pajama bottoms, too. *God, I wish I had two more arms right now.*

As I approach her car she is quite obviously gaping at my pajamas. So much for that. She looks up at me then looks back down at my pj's, then looks up, then back down. I feel the heat burning off my face from embarrassment. She smiles and holds the key out of her car window.

"You were lucky, Mrs. Benson. You called just in the nick of time!"

"Oh, please call me Caroline. I can't thank you enough for doing this."

"No problem! But if you don't mind me asking," she says with a puzzled look, "how is it that you *both* got locked out of the house?"

Oh, here we go. I'm embarrassed enough with my attire and swinging boobalas, I was really hoping to avoid this all together. I honestly didn't think she would ask at this point. I mean, doesn't she have to go back to work? Okay, so she's probably expecting a quick answer. Can this story be shortened? How do you tell someone that a cat locked you out of the house? Okay, like I said before, the truth works best. And I feel I owe her that much after all she's done to help us out of this mess.

"Oh, you are just going to laugh at this one," I say, not sounding so convincing.

"Our cat locked us out! Isn't that silly?"

She had a grin on her face that clearly said she wasn't being told the truth. "I don't understand. How is that possible?"

Okay. Let's face it. You can't really shorten this one. The whole story. Period. "My husband and I were having our coffee outside. Believe it or not, our kitten dropped the pole to the sliding glass door right in it's track. You know those poles. It locked us out. I know it sounds silly, but it's the truth."

"Ah ha. Seriously?" Her smile disappeared and she formed a crease in her eyebrows. Clearly this story sounded absurd to her.

"As implausible as it sounds, do you really think I'd make it up? Do you think I'd come up with such a moronic story while I'm out here talking to you in these plug-ugly pajamas? I'm mortified enough as is. It would have been less embarrassing if I told you that I went to get something out of my car and my husband was throwing something in the mailbox at the same time. And that the front door closed from the wind. Now that story could really happen. My story?" Now I give her a sheepish grin. I threw in a few more details of this mornings train wreck and all she could do was laugh.

"I must say, the story is so hard to believe that there's actually no way it could have been made up so quickly."

Wait! Was I being questioned like a high school student? Was she thinking of disputing my story? Do I have to go to the principal's office?

She gives me a warm smile. I thank her once again and she backs out of the driveway heading back to work. I give her a final wave and walk to my front door. Anxiously, I put the key in the lock. I turn the knob and the door finally opens.

Thank God.

CHAPTER 9

I get to the sliding door in .0000005 seconds flat. Mike jumps up out of the patio chair when he sees me. I pick up the pole with ease and lean it against the refrigerator, making it impossible to fall back on the track. Mittens is weaving in and out of my legs all happy-go-lucky like. I just want to drop-kick her into tomorrow!

I get the door open and Mike just rushes past me to hop straight into the shower. I do the same thing, heading upstairs to the other bathroom.

By the time we are dressed and ready to go to work Mike is making a phone call. He's letting work know that he's on his way. He gives me a kiss, we both whisper 'I love you' and he heads out the door. No other words are exchanged between us.

I turn to the cabinet, grab myself a travel mug and I pour myself a coffee to go.

Just one more simple cup of coffee. I mean, what can it hurt?

EPILOGUE

A couple of people at the office overheard me telling someone why I was late for work. Questions were being thrown at me left and right. After telling my story the first time, there were loud chuckles that couldn't be helped. That brought people over to my desk asking what was so funny, where I would then have to repeat myself. Then more people would stop by who heard about my dilemma through the grapevine and they too had questions and comments as well. By the end of a busy work day, it was clear to me that my story was actually something to laugh about. Maybe Mike is laughing now. We sure as hell weren't laughing this morning, but looking at it all now, it is rather amusing.

I got home around six greeted at the door by Willy, our dog, Seymore, our orange tiger cat, and you guessed it, Mittens. I felt like checking her paws to see if she had anything up her sleeve (or should I say fur). I smiled at the three animals, put my belongings down, and fed the little creatures. Then I went into the fridge and pulled out the chicken that I planned to make for dinner tonight, grabbing the vegetables at the same time. I put the chicken in a lightly oiled frying pan and filled a pot with water to boil. I took a box of rice out of the cupboard.

"Mom!" Alex's loud screaming voice made me jump so high I think my head hit the ceiling.

"Jesus, Al. You scared the crap out of me! What's up, honey? How was your field trip?"

"Mom! What were you thinking? How embarrassing! Everyone at school knows you got locked out of the house and that MS. WELCH had to save you! Seriously? How do you get locked out of the house anyway? How come you didn't have your key? And you ask the SECRETARY to bring it to you? I can't wait for Mike to come home so I can tell HIM what you did! Oh my God!"

Just then Mike walked in the door. "What's all the yelling about?"

I walked over and gave Mike a kiss. "Hi babe. Alex was just asking me how WE got locked out of the house today. Why don't you tell her what happened."

Alex stood there with her arms folded across her chest. "You were BOTH locked out?!"

Mike looked at her with a shit-eaten grin on his face. He was up to no good, I could tell. "Yeah, Al. So you didn't hear how it all happened? It was YOUR cat. Yep. YOUR cat, that I didn't want you to have, that locked your mother and I out of the house. We were having coffee outside and Mittens decided to put the pole in the door to lock us out. And as if that wasn't good enough, she just stood there and laughed at us the entire time."

"Ahhhhhhhhh, haaaaaaaa haaaaaa. No way!" Brian was finding this very humorous. He must have heard the story from the living room. "What really happened?"

Mike glanced back at Alex with a smile. "Oh, I'm not kidding. We tried all the doors and windows to see if you guys left one unlocked as you usually do, but of course not. And there was Mittens, just laughing her ass off thinking this was all just so funny." While Mike was telling the story, he started heading up the stairs. Still, on and on he went telling the story with a hysterical exaggeration that made the story truly seem fake." . . . . and your stupid cat says, *'You guys are such Dumb Asses. Do you want me to take the pole out of the door? Well I'm not. Because you always say I'm not cute'*. That's what she said . . . ."

Mike just kept telling the story until my daughter started laughing. Mike's got a great sense of humor, though you would have never known it after this morning. He must have told the story at work, as I did, and they probably all laughed to make his day as well. We said we would look back at this someday and laugh. We just didn't think it would be so soon.

"No really, Mom. What happened today?"

"Really, guys. It's like Mike said."

We ate dinner and told the story as it really was, which wasn't so far off from what Mike said. They could not believe what happened. They were laughing so hard. At this point, my daughter couldn't wait to tell everyone at school. It was suddenly funny, not embarrassing.

After clearing the table, I turned to everyone and asked, "Does anyone want a cup of coffee?"

Mittens 'meowed'.

Made in United States
North Haven, CT
07 December 2022

28120203R00045